AF583754

AYAIGA: NEIGHBOUR AND HERO

written by **Thomas Higgs**
with **Colin Hall**

illustrated by **Wally Wilfred**

NATIONAL LIBRARY OF AUSTRALIA PUBLISHING

In the remote Roper River region of the Northern Territory more than 110 years ago, an Alawa man committed an act of such exceptional bravery that a King took notice. The man became one of only eight Australian recipients—and the only Indigenous recipient—of the Albert Medal for Gallantry in Saving Life. Today, this medal of bronze, red enamel and red-and-white silk is in Canberra, in the National Library of Australia.

Ayaiga's medal has been assessed as a significant national treasure. Its importance extends beyond its rarity to its historic symbolism. Ayaiga showed humanity, bravery and grace to his white captor, a man who represented a system of dispossession and violence. This was undoubtedly an act worthy of honour, even though the medal is inextricably linked with the colonial settlement that had changed Ayaiga's world.

The National Library is honoured to include Ayaiga's story in its collections, with all of the many lessons it contains.

First Nations Peoples are advised this book contains depictions and names of deceased people, and content that may be distressing.

Mengi mengi nanggaya

Longtime olden time story

Once upon a time, an Alawa man called Ayaiga was living on **watjurndu** (goanna) country near a place called Minyerri. In this part of Australia's far-north, the grassy plains were peppered with termite mounds and hardy old trees, and rocky outcrops formed jagged hills. There were deep billabongs and, in the valleys, where **gayilig-jilig** (springs) flowed, oases of palms and ancient paperbark trees flourished alongside river pandanus.

Ayaiga had a broad pearly white smile and thick shiny black hair. He was not tall but he had broad shoulders and was a **murnda** (solid strong one) for his size. He had learned from his Elders how to care for Country. He was **barmarr** (knowledgeable) and knew how to direct and intervene in the rhythms of nature to make the land fruitful, abounding in **mama** (food) and resources. The Elders had taught him how to use the **warl.ya** (firestick) to cultivate vast tracts of land. He knew the systems and stories to respect and preserve bush tucker. He was also an excellent **ndarn.gi** (tracker) and could read the bush like a book, understanding all the tell-tale signs.

Ayaiga and his family were no longer the only tribe in the bush. There was another group of people and they were hostile and dangerous without cause. This light-skinned tribe had arrived when Ayaiga was a boy and now made their home in the region.

They brought new creatures with them, driving a **yilwuyga** (big mob) of horned beasts from the east, while riding on the backs of wild, big-toothed animals. Neither Ayaiga nor his grandfathers had ever seen these horned beasts, which now grazed the tall grasses of Alawa Country.

Ayaiga was **yagul-nenyi** (frightened) by the **yinangarrwuna** (ghostly) strangers, who carried on as if he and his family were not even there. The family hid themselves at first and always camped as far away as possible. They deliberated on what to call these strange new people and their beasts.

After some time, they realised that these strangers on Country weren't just passing through. Some Alawa people had become inquisitive and started to get to know them. Ayaiga and his family observed that the newcomers were ignorant of their **yangguwan** (secret business/laws and customs) and had no knowledge of the bush. And yet, over the following months, without ever stopping to ask if they could stay, the white men laid claim to the lands of the Alawa.

They busily set up their own camps, constructing huts and fences to mark new boundary lines wherever they felt the need. They cut down trees, used the waterholes and marched to and fro like they owned the place.

Ayaiga learned that these newcomers had given their own names to vast areas of Alawa Country. They had carved the place up into two stations. One was named Hodgson Downs and the other Nutwood Downs. He also discovered that the new horned animals were called 'bullocky' and the proud ones that the men rode on were 'brumbies'.

By the time he was a young man, both stations were becoming well established, but it had come at a cost. To assert authority and scare the Alawa people into compliance there had been many killings for whatever these rifle-wielding newcomers deemed an offence. The laws were mostly invisible to the Alawa people so breaking them was easy. Tensions remained high, even as some of the Alawa men worked for the squatters in exchange for valued items like fishing hooks, blankets, tomahawks, tobacco and food. The squatters didn't want anyone else on their new stations—but they also needed the help.

When Alawa men killed a number of their horses and cattle, it was the perfect excuse for the squatters to exercise their power. They carefully planned their vigilante brand of justice, handing out flour, sugar and tea to the Alawa people, lulling them into a false sense of security. When a number of families had gathered around Hodgson Downs, the squatters took revenge.

As the Alawa men were cutting timber for the station fences, the squatters suddenly surrounded them and opened fire. Once they were all shot dead, the squatters turned on the women and children. It was a bloody massacre. A few lived to tell the story, including one man called Waypuldanya. Thereafter, any cooperation with the squatters meant complying with their absolute power.

Hodgson Downs homestead

Ayaiga and his close family remained defiant. They had not been drawn in by the settlers and so had survived, but they lost many relatives. They became cautious. The massacre had baffled and frightened them. Why had the white men done this terrible thing? But by keeping their distance, they seemed to make the squatters even more guarded and suspicious. The squatters labelled Ayaiga and his family 'the neighbours' because of their presence nearby—without any of the usual neighbourly affection.

Traditional life was increasingly difficult, especially as the new stations occupied some of the best hunting grounds and waterholes. Finding certain bush tucker was harder and harder. The bullocky were also unlike any of the native animals and the landscape wasn't adapted to cope with such large numbers of them trampling the earth. As the mobs wandered all over Country, they interrupted the rhythms and the seasonal patterns of the landscape. Many of the kangaroos and emus Ayaiga usually hunted to feed his family were scared away.

Cattle at a waterhole in the Northern Territory

One day, after a whole morning of **janggay-neni** (hunting), Ayaiga was returning to camp without any bush tucker. He decided to go and look around nearby **Warrigundu** (Hodgson Downs), where the new people occupying his family lands lived. Fortunately, when he arrived, no-one was around and everything was quiet—a possible conflict was avoided for now. He went to look in one of the huts made of roughly cut trees and bark. He gazed for a while, fascinated by all the strange new objects the men had. Then a sack of ground seeds caught his eye. The grains resembled the ground **yarlbun** (waterlily seed) his wife made cakes from, so Ayaiga thought he would use it to feed his hungry family.

Ayaiga photographed in 1912 in East Arnhem Land

On his way back to camp, he came upon one of the big bullocky, standing there in his path chewing grass. He knew the risk he was taking but he was hungry. Bullocky were easy to hunt because they were so slow and lumbering compared to the nimble kangaroos. But bringing them down was a greater challenge. The beast had to be pierced with several **mayalunggu** (hooked-spears) before it was killed. Ayaiga managed it and in no time at all he was carving the animal up, taking all the best-looking cuts. When he returned to camp, he had **gumbi** (meat) and a bag of ground grains to make into cakes. Together the family made a fire and **garr-angana** (roasted) everything in the coals.

They all tucked in, noting the sweetness of the roasted ribs and the similarity between the new seed cakes and traditional **yarlbun** (waterlily seed) damper. Of the **gumbi** (beef), there was a back-leg part, rump-steaks and sweet tasting rib-bones. That night the family were all **birl-nemberli** (full stomach/ satisfied with food) and everyone praised Ayaiga for his courage in the face of these invaders. But big trouble was coming.

Waterlily

Mounted Constable William Francis Johns, a **junggurn** (without a mate/single) South Australian, was second in charge at Leichhardt's Bar Police Station on the Roper River. He was completing his agreement of five years of service on Australia's far northern frontier. Leichhardt's Bar was named after the explorer Ludwig Leichhardt. Johns had heard a rumour that Leichhardt was last seen crossing the Roper River at the 'bar' and, once across into the wild lands beyond, was never seen or heard from again. He hoped he didn't meet the same fate.

Leichhardt's Bar was a geological formation dividing the river into two distinct levels. It was almost 100 kilometres from the sea to the bar and it was possible to navigate all the way to it, making it an ideal place for a police station. Heading inland, the river continued a further 190 kilometres—as isolated from what he called 'civilised life' as he could possibly imagine. Johns' duties at Leichhardt's Bar Police Station included patrolling the various cattle stations of the region and protecting the interests of the squatters by upholding the laws of the Crown.

Signing up to work for the Northern Territory Police Force was a rite of passage for troopers from South Australia, especially if they were ambitious. However, in that year, 1911, the Northern Territory's administration had been transferred to the Commonwealth Government, so Johns now received his orders from Melbourne.

William Francis Johns, at about 24 years old

Word had reached the police station at Leichhardt's Bar of 'an incident' at Hodgson Downs. Johns was sent to capture the guilty party and bring them in. He knew of the troubles they'd had at Hodgson Downs in the past and he was determined to get there before the station owners took the law into their own hands.

As Johns got closer to the claimed pastoral lease, he came across more and more cattle. They were fat at this time of year as the wet season rains had transformed the country into a green sea of tall grass. The station was situated on some of the best country he had been through. He could see how conflicts would arise. Johns camped along the way and arrived in the morning after a few days' trek.

On arrival, the mounted constable was greeted by irate squatters, who barraged him with ranting and raving about his duties as a copper. Johns asked the squatters what they knew about the suspect and then set off in pursuit, with backup from a squatter who claimed he had witnessed the theft from the hut. They headed in the direction in which the squatters had seen bush camps in the past and, after half a day's walk, they got lucky when smoke was sighted from a smouldering campfire.

They hid their horses and crawled about 100 metres through the long grass. As the two men got closer, they found that the campground was empty so they waited in ambush. After about an hour, they could hear a family returning to camp from the opposite direction. The group was singing and calling out in glee after a fun time hunting and gathering bush tucker. The women had **minjarrbi** (dillybags) full of **yarragaga** (bush-black currant) and **mbagarr** (honeycomb) from native bees. The boys were carrying a huge dead **watjurndu** (goanna). They had no idea what was lying in wait.

Suddenly, the two men charged into the camp pointing their rifles. The squatter immediately went for Ayaiga and called to Johns, 'This is the one!' Johns let off a gunshot into the air to frighten the others and joined his companion in overpowering Ayaiga. As one held him down, the other secured handcuffs and then a chain with a padlock around his neck.

With the accused restrained, Johns surveyed the area and soon found a sack labelled 'Flour'. There were also some charred rib-bones at the edge of the fire, which confirmed that Ayaiga was a poacher and a thief. In the eyes of the white-man's law, Ayaiga had been caught red-handed. He was led away by the men who had accused him of **ngenyi-neni** (stealing)—men who were squatting without consent on Alawa Country. '**Nyingaya ngaba-barra** (I'm worried for my Country)!' he called to his family.

As the squatter returned to his hut, Johns mounted his horse and began to march the barefooted Ayaiga back through the valley to the police station at Leichhardt's Bar. From there, Ayaiga expected to be taken away, tried and judged, and most likely sentenced to work, breaking rocks in a prison labour camp. But, for now, they were still in the bush.

Johns and Ayaiga could not understand each other so they marched **ngarl-manyja-wanda** (not talking). The **wirr-narla** (walk) was tough going, especially for Ayaiga, who had to keep up with the horse and follow Johns' clumsy route through the scrub. If he fell behind, the chain would yank his neck, sometimes dragging him to the ground. Ayaiga knew the best way to go but Johns **wungun** (didn't understand) when Ayaiga attempted to guide him, such was his distrust of his captive.

And so it was that they arrived at a **nanggurru** (salt-water crocodile) infested creek in full flood—the worst possible place **law-narla** (to cross). His petitions to head upstream to a safer place fell upon deaf ears as the stubborn constable insisted they press on through the **marraman** (floodwater).

Johns released the neck chain to allow Ayaiga to hold it for the crossing, but didn't undo the padlock from around his neck. Ayaiga looped up the slack and held it over his shoulder. Johns dismounted and the two men entered the water on either side of the horse, leaning in to its saddle for balance. They started off reasonably well but as they went deeper it became harder and harder, and soon all three were struggling

The many-braided channels of the Roper River are often in flood, as here in 1914

to find their footing. In the middle of the stream, they were swept off their feet and the horse began to panic under the weight of the saddle bags.

All of a sudden, the horse was upturned by the swell and, with its legs flailing wildly, it kicked Johns in the head, knocking him into a semi-conscious state. As Johns floated off downstream, Ayaiga made it across the river by using the weight of his chain as ballast. The extra stability had enabled him to half-swim and half-climb on submerged branches through the fastest part of the stream. But having reached the bank, he looked back to see the limp body of the policeman caught up in the top leaves of flooded **ruwana** (pandanus) palms.

Without thinking twice about his own welfare, and still holding the weighty chain, Ayaiga dived back into the deep **marraman** (floodwater). He managed to **jad-najini** (catch) the **ngawurr-arrganya** (drowning) man just in time and, with all his strength, began to haul Johns' lifeless body through the floodwaters. Ayaiga was often forced under by the weight of the tall policeman but he kept going until finally his feet could touch the bottom. Catching his breath, Ayaiga dragged Johns' body up onto the bank. Johns came back to his senses and reached for his pounding head. A huge egg had come up from the horse's blow. He soon realised what had happened and that he owed his life to the man who sat, exhausted, at his side. Still in shock, and overwhelmed by the whole event, Johns fell back into unconsciousness.

When Johns finally awoke, he was surprised to see that his prisoner hadn't tried to escape but was in fact waiting for him to come to. Ayaiga had retrieved the horse, which was also lucky to **wanyma** (be alive). The horse had been washed across the river some distance further downstream. The saddle bags were still there but everything was sodden and spoiled. In another act of incredible **murrja-neni** (kindness) towards the wounded constable, Ayaiga helped him back into the saddle and led him the rest of the way to Roper River, this time following the safest and easiest route.

As Johns began to make sense of what had just happened, he reflected on the man who had saved his life. 'He has valued my life as much as his own!' remarked Johns, finishing his thinking out loud. 'I shall call you Neighbour!' He continued to make clear his intention by pointing at Ayaiga and repeating, 'Neighbour!'

Ayaiga (third from left) and Johns (left) at Leichhardt's Bar Police Station

From this point on, whenever Johns addressed Ayaiga, or mentioned him in reports or anecdotes, he called him Neighbour. And so it was that Ayaiga became known to the white people as Neighbour. Once they arrived at Leichhardt's Bar Police Station, Ayaiga's neck chain was linked to a string of other arrested tribesmen. Mounted Constable Johns was second in charge at Leichhardt's Bar under Trooper Kelly, who had also been busy on patrols. All the men, from other nation groups of the region, had fallen foul of the superimposed legal system of the white man. From here, they embarked on a two-week forced march through the bush to faraway law courts on unknown Country. The captives were led in a long train towards the settlement of Pine Creek, with the now-recovered Johns as official police escort.

Police awaiting their arrival took the men straight to the gaol. Here the prisoner's chains were attached to steel loops set into the rock floors of the dank rooms, where they were left awaiting trial. Ayaiga's first night chained to the floor was the worst. In the space of a few weeks, his entire life had been turned upside down: from the wide open country of his homeland, with a bounty of resources at his disposal, to an empty cell. During one of the long days of waiting, Ayaiga had an unexpected visit from Johns, who came to give him some cakes, which supplemented his meagre ration of prison food. The roasted cakes tasted the same as the ones his wife had made with the squatters' grain. Ayaiga smiled in appreciation.

Although the timber at Pine Creek was of excellent quality, it was not the pines that had transformed the place into a bustling settlement, but the gold discovered in its waters. Ayaiga watched the hive of activity through his barred cell window. It was here that he first saw another newcomer to the land. These people were unlike the white men in character, generally shorter in stature and distinctly different in appearance. Their clothes and hats were new to Ayaiga and some wore their black hair in long woven ropes, trailing down their backs. There were twenty of them for every white man.

One of them was more interested in observing the street action than being involved with it. He sat in the shade not far from the prison waving a brush in beautiful strokes across semi-transparent white sheets. Ayaiga could see just enough to work out that the man was **miljirr-enyunu** (painting) and it reminded him of his grandfather's paintings up in the rock-shelters of the **ganjanjarra** (stone country). Watching the man paint was a welcome distraction from the desperation of the claustrophobic cell.

A Chinese gold miner at Pine Creek, 1917

Miners including Chinese carriers at Pine Creek, 1912

When the day of his trial finally arrived, Ayaiga was taken to the courthouse, where charges of larceny were laid. 'We call Neighbour to the stand!' said the judge. The judge's job was not to execute justice but to protect the interests of the invading squatters. The ruling was a foregone conclusion—until Mounted Constable Johns stood up to address the courtroom.

Surprising all present, Johns spoke in defence of Ayaiga, saying that he had no solid proof to back the larceny charges, even if evidence was not usually required to convict a 'native' prisoner. But when Johns began to relay the events of how Ayaiga had saved his life, everyone was stunned. The story challenged all of their prejudices. As a result of Johns' testimony, all of the charges were dropped and 'Neighbour' was free to go. 'Well, what could I do?' Johns later reflected. 'How could I remain silent and see this man sentenced to life behind bars, after what he had done for me?'

The story of Ayaiga's bravery spread throughout the town, then far and wide on the overland telegraph, until it reached the ears of Bishop Lefroy, all the way down south in Melbourne. The bishop shared the story with the head of his order in London, the Archbishop of Canterbury. As the highest-ranking civilian outside the British royal family, the archbishop reported to none other than His Majesty the King, George V.

The King was fascinated by the tale, which played into the myth of the noble savage living in the wilderness of outback Australia. He also saw the political opportunity to paint—in whitewash—a positive picture of the happenings on the far frontiers of the empire. The King decreed, and all agreed, that the native called 'Neighbour' should be awarded the Albert Medal, named after the King's very own grandfather. The medal, 'For Gallantry in Saving Life on Land', was the highest award a civilian anywhere in the vast British Empire could receive.

Oblivious to the talk of the settlers and their decorations, and motivated by his deep longing to be back with his family, Ayaiga had made the 320-kilometre journey home **wirr-narla** (go on foot)—his eyes now wide open to the extent of the white man's reach. Ayaiga's family were overjoyed at his unexpected return. He recounted the events at the flooded creek to everyone's amazement. They celebrated in song and with tears of joy all night.

Ayaiga at Roper River, 1928

Over the following weeks, Ayaiga surveyed his lands. He keenly observed the **werneju-enu** (spoil something/ make it go bad) impact of all the new animals and the pollution of waterholes around the squatters' permanent camps. It continued to be challenging to find sustainable amounts of bush tucker, as the marauding cattle disrupted the regular patterns of native animals. Ayaiga's options were few. Traditional life was no longer possible in the same way and he knew all too well the possible consequences of crossing these invaders.

When Mounted Constable Johns showed up again seeking his help as a tracker in exchange for rations— and, more importantly, protection from the squatters— Ayaiga took him up on the offer. After the trial, Johns had travelled back from Pine Creek to continue his posting at Leichhardt's Bar Police Station. He had had a change of heart towards Aboriginal people in the wake of Neighbour's arrest. There was a need for Aboriginal trackers at Leichhardt's Bar and Johns could think of no person he would rather have as his offsider than Neighbour. And so, for a second time, he had gone in search of Neighbour.

Mounted Police (Johns at left in middle row) with Aboriginal trackers and house staff, 1910

Ayaiga's 'pay' sometimes included a blanket, tinned meat and tobacco but it was usually just flour, sugar and tea leaves. Johns wanted Ayaiga to stay at Leichhardt's Bar but Ayaiga and his family moved to a hill nearby called Walunji to remain on traditional Alawa Country. He showed Johns where to find him and, whenever there was work, Johns would bring him back to assist.

It came as a great surprise to Ayaiga when word arrived **ngalbinjiyunu** (from a long way away) that the invaders wanted to bestow a high honour upon him. An entire dry season had been and gone and the new rainy season was in full swing when he set off to Port Darwin to receive the award.

This time he rode one of the police horses—a skill he had now mastered—to Leichhardt's Bar, where he boarded a wooden supply ship and sailed downstream into the Gulf of Carpentaria. The ship then took him north around Cape Arnhem and the Wessel Islands, west across the Arafura Sea, and down through Van Diemen's Gulf to Port Darwin.

The feeling of the salty air blowing across the vast open water etched itself upon Ayaiga's memory. The **marlurrulurru** (sea) voyage was exhilarating, unlike anything he had experienced. Along the way, the vessel stopped at other outposts, where there were yet more white men with Aboriginal prisoners, who were loaded aboard in chains for various violations against the interests of the settlers. After half an **ardangarri** (lunar) cycle at sea, the ship finally arrived in Port Darwin.

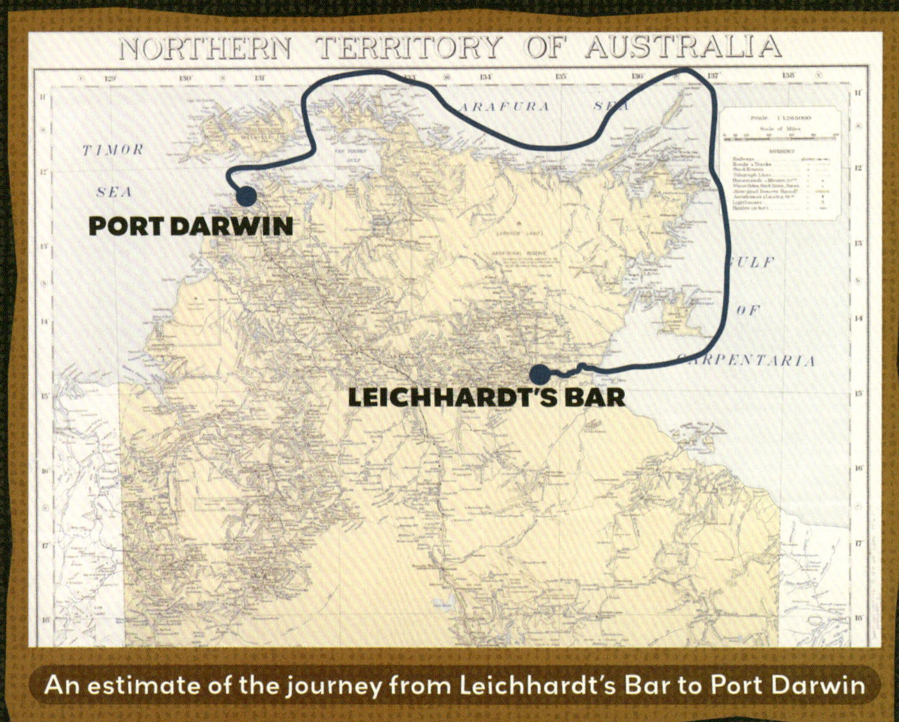

An estimate of the journey from Leichhardt's Bar to Port Darwin

Port Darwin in 1912, with Government House on the hill at right

On a typically hot and humid December day, in the year 1912, Ayaiga was taken to Government House. He had been given a khaki police uniform and some shiny black shoes especially for the occasion. The stone house with its seven-pointed roof was the grandest of the newcomers' buildings that Ayaiga had seen.

Just before the sun was at its peak, the 50 or so people who had gathered were ushered into the drawing room. In a stream of foreign proceedings, which Ayaiga understood to be a form of ceremony, men stood up and read speeches. Each acknowledged that it was the first time an act of heroism by an Aboriginal person had been recognised. They spoke of Ayaiga's exceptional courage and his willingness to risk his own personal safety to save his captor. This defied the common expectations of the era, they said.

Ayaiga wearing his medal at Government House

The front and reverse of Ayaiga's medal

Ayaiga listened as they spoke about 'natives' and 'children of nature' and 'savages'. Although the language was mostly unknown to Ayaiga, the speakers' gestures made it clear that a graphic account was being given of that day on the flooded river with Mounted Constable Johns and his horse.

Finally, Ayaiga was invited to come forward and receive the award, 'Presented in the name of His Majesty King George V to Neighbour, an Aboriginal native of the Roper River, for gallantry in saving life on February 1st 1911'. He heard the crowd's applause as the little oval object was fastened to his police tunic. A man disappeared beneath a black cloth and a flash of light exploded to photograph the occasion.

Ayaiga returned home without his medal—which would be kept in Darwin on his behalf—but with its red-and-white ribbon. He was now a hero in two cultures. He and **yilngababarra** (my Country people) would continue to live alongside their new neighbours on Alawa Country, **watjurndu** (goanna) and **ganjanjarra** (stone country), showing bravery and gallantry every day.

Author's note

I first heard the story of 'Neighbour' on the radio. Knowing the value of such stories, I did not forget it and soon incorporated it into my teaching program in Marrara, Darwin, on Larrakia Country.

Local historian and storyteller Don Christophersen had been remembering the forgotten heroes of the Northern Territory for decades. Using his research, students were able to read reports of Ayaiga's bravery from the time and consider the story from different perspectives.

The story was a source of pride for the Indigenous students, who loved discovering their own hero. After a few years, I had some Alawa students in my class who already knew the story. It had been passed down through their oral tradition of storytelling. I was invited to visit one of the students in their homeland of Minyerri during the school holidays. The following year, the student's relative came through my class and produced a picture of two men with Ayaiga's Albert Medal. Pointing at one of the men, he said, 'That's my dad!' I was amazed that I was teaching a direct descendent of Ayaiga. What an honour!

As Don Christophersen says, 'Neighbour led an extraordinary life. If it was another type of person, a non-Aboriginal person, who had won this medal for bravery, it would have been well written about but it seemed to just fade into dust. It needed someone to bring it back to life'. And it is thanks to Don's work that you are reading this story now.

Thomas Higgs

From Ayaiga's grandson

I'm happy and proud to be here, seeing all the wonderful faces. We are all here today because of one man and what he did. The bravery and heart. What he did—it was for a purpose, it was for this day, it was to bring us together.

I'm an Alawa man. I've learned from my dad, from my grandfathers and they have learned from their fathers: our land was given to us from generation to generation to generation; it was given to us through our Aboriginal Dreamtime story and history. I'm connected to my land, to my people, to the Dreaming. My body's got a skin name.

Before we came, my dad cried because he knew what we were coming up here for—it was for the medal, the bravery of my grandfather. It will be passed on to my kids and their kids. And we'll be sharing and holding hands, we'll be working together, shoulder to shoulder. We will always carry what this man did.

That man was a hero to me. I know my grandfathers; they were like warriors. And still today my people are carrying on and helping. There are a lot of wonderful people doing amazing things, night and day, every day. One day, it'll be your kids doing the greatest thing for the future. For my people back home, that will be the most wonderful thing.

And it's like taking my grandfather back home, where his message will be for the future. You will see him through the eyes of his grandchildren like me. I'm happy to be here and thank you!

Edited extract from a speech by Darren Farrell
Alawa Traditional Owner and Custodian of Ayaiga's Albert Medal

My connection

My connection to the story of Ayaiga pulses through my veins in a way many would never expect. First, I must begin with a crucial fact: I am Gurindji. My people, for time immemorial, have nurtured the unforgiving landscapes of the central western desert. So, it came as a surprise to me that my connection to Ayaiga was through his balanda (white) oppressor.

In my family we rarely spoke of William Johns. He was neither present nor relevant in our storytelling. Our Aboriginal matriarchs have always sat at the centre of the universe. These are the characters who mattered for us. So, in hearing the story of Ayaiga as a child, I thought our connection was through the Aboriginal man, the hero; this was the only way it could make sense. How could our Aboriginal family be connected to the white man? To the man who was serving an injustice?

Johns certainly had a family of his own down south. But during his time as a police officer in the Northern Territory (and this was not uncommon) he contributed to a few other families—and by 'contributed', I mean he fathered illegitimate children with Aboriginal women. William Johns happened to father my Nanna and her sister during one of his policing expeditions to Kalkarindji. Nanna was raised by her mother and clan, next to a waterhole, until she was 8 years old. It was at this point that she became a member of the Stolen Generation, when Australia deemed her a 'half-caste' and incarcerated her in a compound 800 kilometres away from her people.

Through tracking the movements of Johns on his journey around the Territory, we can see that his near-drowning occurred before his time in Kalkarindji. From that, we can assume that if Ayaiga had not saved his oppressor, then my entire family may never have existed.

It is not my place to comment on or attempt to answer whether or not Ayaiga did the 'right' thing in saving Johns. This question, in my opinion, is not one that should even be asked. I do not wish to tell Aboriginal people, especially of Ayaiga's era, what the 'correct' reaction to oppression is and was. What I can say is that Ayaiga demonstrated humanity in a way that was seldom afforded to us—and for that he is a hero.

Emma King

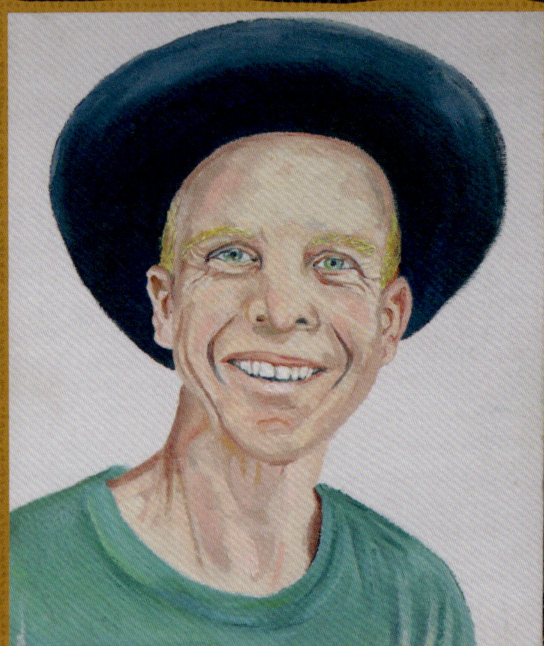

Thomas Higgs is a teacher and award-winning portrait artist living in Darwin. He enjoys painting, gardening and visiting friends in remote communities across the Northern Territory. Thomas uses portraiture to tell stories and honour the lives of his subjects. He would like to see all Australians learning about our rich First Nations history and culture and regards collaboration like this book as an act of reconciliation.

Wally Wilfred is an artist living and working in the Roper River region, who works with the Ngukurr Art Centre. Wally brings together traditional techniques with bold and contemporary use of colour. Wally's work explores traditional and present-day culture with history and storytelling, sometimes about the effect colonisation has had on his people and Country.

Darren Farrell

Emma King

Colin Hall

Don Christophersen

Glossary

The Ngukurr Language Centre is a small not-for-profit organisation in southern Arnhem Land. Alawa man Colin Hall from the Roper River region works at the centre supporting the teaching of Kriol and working to revive the endangered Alawa language of his ancestors. Colin and the community language workers at Ngukurr produced this glossary, which includes Kriol, the main language spoken in Ngukurr today.

Alawa	English	Kriol
ardangarri	lunar	mun
barmarr	knowledgeable	sabibala
birl-nemberli	satisfied with food	bulap binji
ganjanjarra	stone country	stoun kantri
garr-angana	roasted	roustim
gayilig-jilig	springs	springwada
gumbi	meat/beef	bip
jad-najini	catch	gajim
janggay-neni	hunting	hanting
junggurn	without a mate/single	singgul
law-narla	to cross (a river)	wok langa woda
mama	food	daga
marlurrulurru	sea	solwoda
marraman	floodwater	fladawada
mayalunggu	hooked-spears	barragarl
mbagarr	honeycomb	jugubeg
miljirr-enyunu	painting	peinting
minjarrbi	dillybags	dilibeg

Alawa	English	Kriol
murnda	solid strong one	strongbalawan
murrja-neni	kindness	ngutjurrwan
nanggurru	salt-water crocodile	aligida
ndarn.gi	tracker	treka
ngalbinjiyunu	from a long way away	longwei kantri
ngarl-manyja-wanda	not talking	jidan kwait
ngawurr-arrganya	drowning	draunt
ngenyi-neni	stealing	stilim
nyingaya ngaba-barra	I'm worried for my Country	nyingaya bla main kantri
ruwana	pandanus	pendemis
wanyma	be alive	laibala
warl.ya	firestick	faiyastik
Warrigundu	Hodgson Downs Station	Warrigundu
watjurndu	goanna	gowena
werneju-enu	spoil something	meigi nugud
wirr-narla	walk/go on foot	futwok
wungun	didn't understand	nomo sabi
yagul-nenyi	frightened	atjamp
yangguwan	secret business/ laws and customs	nyukurrwan
yarlbun	waterlily-seeds	yarlbun
yarragaga	bush-black currant	tjupi
yilngababarra	my Country people	kantriman
yilwuyga	big mob	bigismob
yinangarrwuna	ghostly	debuldebul

For Minyerri and the Alawa people - TH

Image credits: **p.10** *Northern Territory—Homestead Hodgson Downs*, 1924–1935, NAA, M4435, 508; **p.11** *Cattle at a waterhole (Kalkarindji)*, 1920, L&A NT, PH0357/0029; **p.14** Sir Walter Baldwin Spencer, *Ayaiga (Neighbour), winner of the Albert Medal, Roper River ...*, 1912, MV, XP 15456; **p.15** Ellis Rowan, *Nymphaea violacea Lehm.*, c.1911, NLA, nla.obj-138783516; **p.17** *William Francis Johns*, c.1909, SLSA, B 20181; **p.20** *Roper River in flood*, 1914, L&A NT, PH0734/0069; **p.24** *Leichhardt's Bar lock-up*, 1914, L&A NT, PH0734/0022; **p.28** Walter Herbert Bradshaw, *Chinese carrier*, 1917, L&A NT, PH0856/0030; **p.29** J.P. Campbell, *Carriers*, 1912, L&A NT, PH0100/0094; **p.31** Dr Herbert Basedow, [Film negative—*Neighbour*], 1928, NMA, 1985.0060.1475.001; **p.33** *Police*, 1910, L&A NT, PH0188/0114; **p.34** Department of the Interior, *Northern Territory of Australia*, c.1941, NLA, nla.obj-567078164; **p.35** J.P. Campbell, *Darwin from Stokes Hill*, 1912, NLA, nla.obj-146751366; **p.36** *Portrait of Aya-I-Ga*, 1911, NLA, nla.obj-145920152; **p.37** *Albert Medal presented to Aya-I-Ga*, 1911, NLA, nla.obj-139608611.

Published by
National Library of Australia Publishing
Canberra ACT 2600

ISBN: 9781922507785

Alawa and Kriol language has been shared in this book courtesy of Colin Hall and the Ngukurr Language Centre.

The National Library of Australia acknowledges Australia's First Nations Peoples—the First Australians—as the Traditional Owners and Custodians of this land and gives respect to the Elders—past and present—and through them to all Australian Aboriginal and Torres Strait Islander people.

Publisher: Lauren Smith
Managing editor: Amelia Hartney
Designer: Keisha Leon of Cause/Affect
Image coordinators: Madeleine Warburton and Jessica Wallace

Printed in China on FSC®-certified paper by C&C Offset Printing Co., Ltd.

Find out more about NLA Publishing at library.gov.au/discover/nla-publishing.

A catalogue record for this book is available from the National Library of Australia.